SCOTT A. SMITH'S
SERIOUS BLUES

ESSENTIAL PHRASING

MW01260130

GET YOUR FINGERS TO PLAY
WHAT'S IN YOUR HEAD

Alfred Music
P.O. Box 10003
Van Nuys, CA 91410-0003
alfred.com

ISBN-10: 1-4706-1116-3 (Book & DVD)
ISBN-13: 978-1-4706-1116-3 (Book & DVD)

Cover Photos
Fender Select Stratocaster® courtesy of Fender Musical Instruments Corporation
Texture: © iStockphoto / ARENA Creative • Scrollwork: © iStockphoto / Gintaras Svalbonas • Road: © iStockphoto / Mlenny Photography

 Alfred Cares. Contents printed on environmentally responsible paper.

CONTENTS

INTRODUCTION

If you have been playing long enough to feel limited by what you know and what your fingers can do, the Serious Blues series is for you. You have developed some lead guitar chops and know some scales and chords, but would like to be able to play like the killer blues artists you've heard. Each book and DVD package in this series features a monster blues guitarist teaching the techniques and musical concepts you need to become an authentic blues musician. You'll be learning from the best and will be inspired by the amazing demonstrations of licks and exercises in the video.

The optimum learning experience with the Serious Blues series is to watch the video, guitar in hand ready to play, with the book open in front of you. Example numbers will be displayed on your television or computer screen, directing you to licks and exercises in the book that include standard music notation, TAB, and chord or scale fretboard diagrams. Stop the video at any time to practice an example. To ensure the effectiveness of the training offered here, master each lick or exercise before continuing on to the next lesson.

To make it easier for you to choose the appropriate Serious Blues book and DVD package, they have been categorized into levels that are explained below.

ESSENTIAL

This level assumes you can read TAB and/or standard music notation, and know how to read chord and scale fretboard diagrams. You know all of the basic open-position chords and are ready for barres and other movable chords. You have some familiarity with the pentatonic scale and are ready to learn a number of alternate positions in which it can be played. You're ready to master fundamental techniques like hammer-ons, pull-offs, alternate picking, and even some more specialized techniques, such as bending, trills, rakes, and slides. In addition, you are ready to work with concepts like targeting chord tones, phrasing, and constructing a solo over a 12-bar blues progression. You also have the music theory background needed to begin learning the modes of the major scale and incorporate them into your soloing.

EXPANDING

To begin at this level, you should have all the skills and knowledge developed at the ESSENTIAL level and are ready to explore more intermediate techniques and concepts. You have the musical understanding needed to learn all the different types of 7th chords, plus extended and altered chords in a variety of voicings. You're ready for basic applications of vibrato, harmonics, fingerstyle, and hybrid picking, as well as concepts like call and response, fills between vocals, and a variety of shuffle styles and blues forms.

Tune Up

In the DVD menu, select Tuning. It will take you to a page where you will hear an audio track that will play each string several times, starting with the 1st string, high E. Compare your strings to this audio track to get in tune with the DVD.

BENDING AND THE A MINOR PENTATONIC SCALE

One of the most exciting and dynamic techniques in blues guitar has to be the art of *bending* strings. Nothing tugs at the soul like the wailing and crying of a slow, tortured blues solo. Over the next couple of lessons, we will explore this important topic. We will also take some time along the way to learn some fierce, bending licks. In this lesson, we will address the technique and ear training required to create this gut-wrenching sound. We will also learn some of the most widely used bends using our favorite blues pattern, the A Minor Pentatonic Box #1.

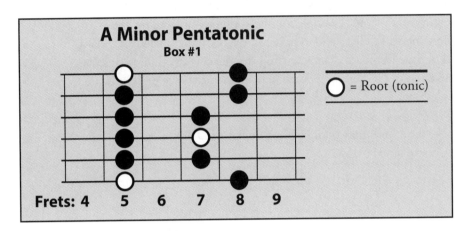

How to Bend

When we bend a note, we're actually playing a specific note and pushing or stretching that note up in pitch to arrive precisely at a different note.

Left-hand finger: 3

The bend to the left is referred to as a *whole-step bend*, meaning that the string is stretched up in pitch one *whole step*, or the distance of two frets. Note that a whole-step bend is indicated with an arrow and the number "1" above it. This is an extremely important bend to master. There are many different types of bends, but let's conquer this one first.

Bending can be hard on the hands. We have to make sure we're using the proper blues-bending grip. We do this for maximum leverage and stamina. When we bend, it's a good idea to let the thumb hang over the top of the neck. This helps stabilize our hand and provide added leverage. Let's use our 3rd finger to fret the note that we intend to bend, and let our 1st and 2nd finger follow closely behind. This provides extra muscle. The three fingers and the thumb work together to squeeze out the bend.

The Whole-Step Bend

It takes a while to develop the muscle required for good bending technique, so be patient with your hands and do not overwork them. It also takes a while to train your ear to hear the pitches you are bending to, so be patient with your ears as well. In the next exercise, we're going to play a few whole-step bends in different areas on the neck, just to see how it feels and sounds. Remember to listen closely and use your blues-bending grip.

For this exercise, we'll also employ some *right-hand muting* to stop the sound of the bent note. Right-hand muting is accomplished by touching the side of the palm of your right hand against the strings in order to stop the vibration of the string. This technique can be utilized in many different ways, but in this case we will use it to stop the sound of the bent note so that the sound of the bend being released isn't heard.

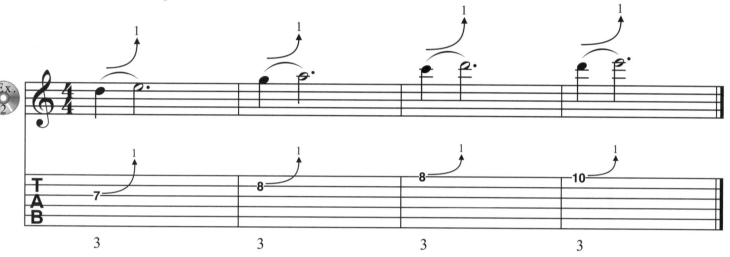

After you've played the exercise a couple of times, try playing the whole-step bend anywhere and everywhere on the neck. Concentrate on training your ear to hear the whole step precisely. Be creative and have fun.

Initial and Destination Notes

Now that we've found some useful places to bend, let's discuss how to use our ears to hear them. First off, bends of this type have two components: the *initial note* and the *destination note*. We start out by playing the initial note, and then we bend and use our ears to hear the pitch of the destination note.

Initial Note   Destination Note

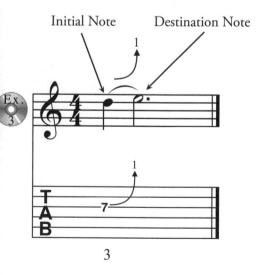

Following is a great method to teach our ears how to hear specific bent pitches.

First, play the
initial note.

Then, slide up and play the
destination note.

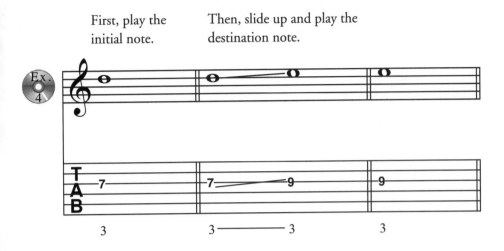

Let the destination note sink into your ears and really hear it. Now, while that note is still fresh
in your head, go back to the initial note and bend it to match the pitch you're hearing.

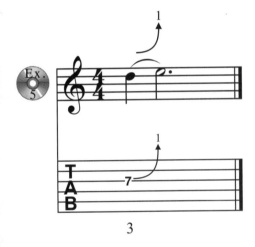

Try this on your own, all over the neck. Make a game out of it and see how many pitches you
can nail in a row.

In this next exercise, we'll use a similar approach, but in a more musical context. Try to keep the A Minor Pentatonic Box #1 in mind as we play this exercise. Let's try it together and concentrate on pitch.

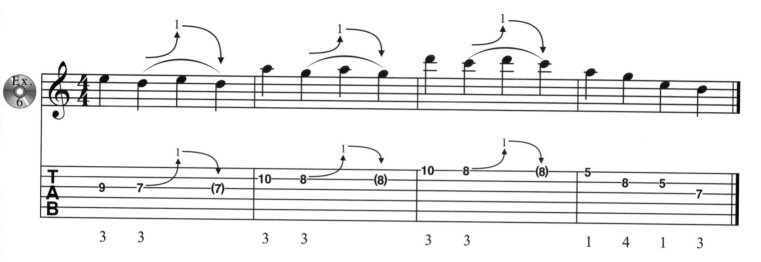

Combining Bends with Box Pattern

Let's get bluesy and learn how to combine our bends with the notes in the A Minor Pentatonic Box #1 to create some mighty tasty blues licks.

Our first lick features an *eighth-note triplet* on beat 1. A triplet consists of three notes in the time of two notes of the same value. So, in this case, three eighth notes are to be played in the time of two eighth notes, or one beat.

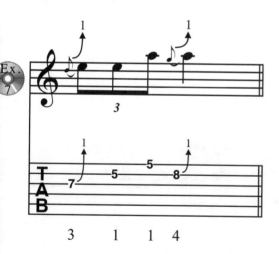

Notice how we have to anchor our 1st finger and bend with the other two fingers, and then jump up and grab the bend at the 2nd string. Our proper fingerings get pushed aside when bending. We always use the strongest fingers first, even if it means breaking protocol. But by all means, experiment with this and try different fingers.

In the lick below, notice how all of the notes come out of our box pattern.

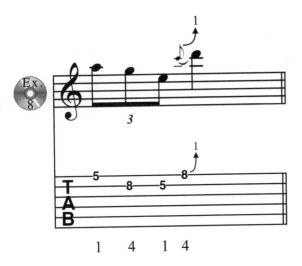

Let's check out another lick. It starts out just like the last one, but look out for the cool triplet on beat 2!

In the next exercise, we'll combine our three licks to create a saucy blues statement.

Remember to use the blues grip and hear the destination pitch in your head.

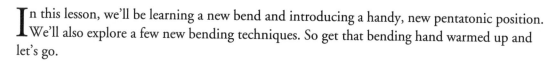

HALF-STEP BENDS

In this lesson, we'll be learning a new bend and introducing a handy, new pentatonic position. We'll also explore a few new bending techniques. So get that bending hand warmed up and let's go.

The Half-Step Bend

By now, you're probably getting pretty good at bending up a whole step. Now that we have that one together, let's learn a new one. A *half-step bend* is approached exactly like a whole-step bend except we bend the note a half step instead of a whole step, or the distance of one fret instead of two. Note that a half-step bend is indicated by an arrow with a "½" above it.

Let's use our ear-training exercise from the previous lesson to play a few half-step bends.

First, play the initial note D.

Then slide up and play the destination note E♭.

Now, go back to the initial note and bend.

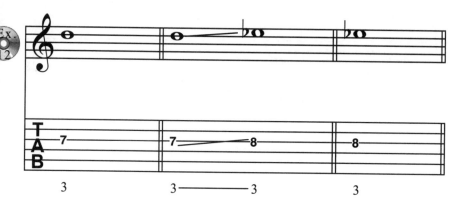

Another Half-Step Bend

Next, we'll play a great repeating lick that features the half-step bend and the following notes from Box #1 of the A Minor Pentatonic scale. (Note: a *blue note* is a lowered 3rd, 5th, or 7th degree of the major scale that helps create the characteristic sound of the blues. The blue note below is a lowered 5th.)

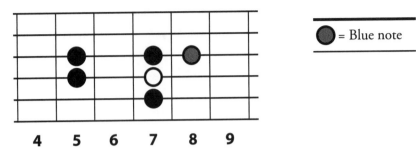

This exercise also utilizes *Swing 8ths*, an extremely common performance practice in blues and jazz. It means that eighth notes should not be played evenly, but rather as a triplet divided into a quarter note and an eighth note.

This: Should be played like this:

In the exercise below, we will bend in tempo and let the note rise and fall in pitch without cutting it off. This is known as *bend and release*.

Box-Jumping Lick with Bends

Let's try this cool exercise, which starts out with the following lick.

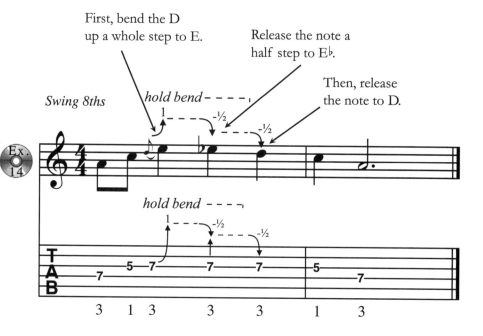

Now, let's move this lick higher on the fretboard.

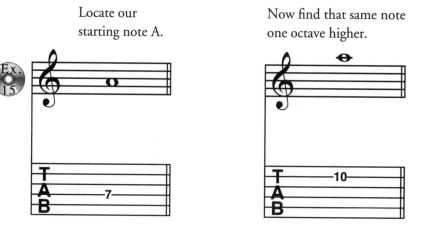

Starting from that note, transfer the lick by its shape to the new location on the neck. This gives us the exact notes one octave higher.

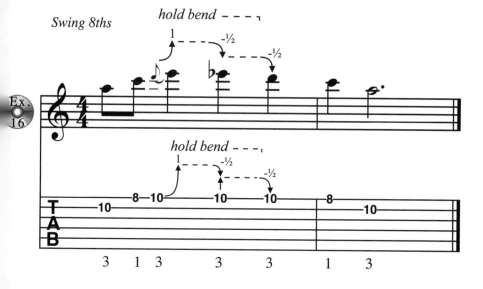

Not only do we get two licks for the price of one, but we've also stumbled into the territory of the A Minor Pentatonic Box #2. It's a good idea to memorize this piece of the pattern and the bendable note at the 10th fret of the 1st string.

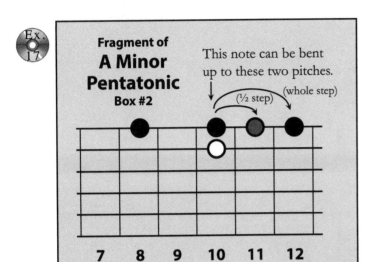

When you couple the above pattern fragment to our Box #1 pattern, you'll have a vast playground of licks and potential bends. Now, let's combine our two licks and play this exercise.

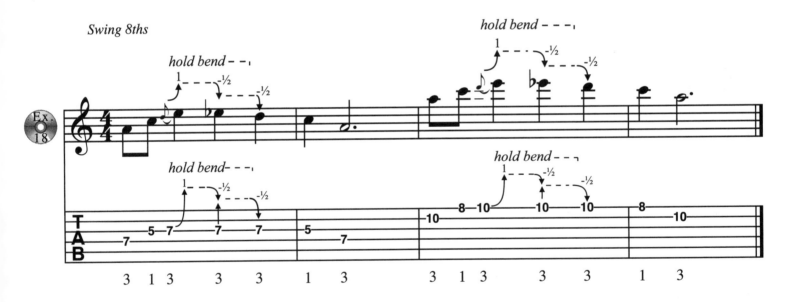

Bending Licks That Rule

Now, let's put some of this stuff together with a few licks. Our first lick is a great-sounding whole-step bend

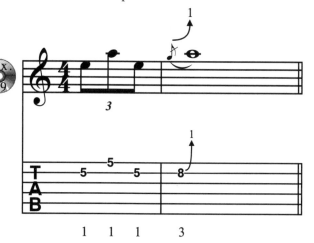

The next lick uses the half-step bend to get to the blue note. Notice that we bend the note before we pick it. This is called *pre-bending* a note. Bend, play it, and release it to the next pitch.

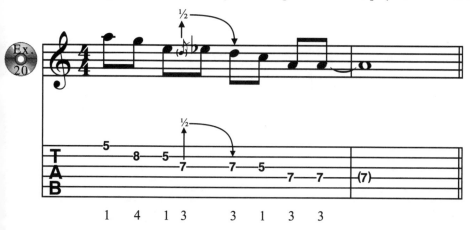

Our last lick rockets up into Box #2 for a classic blues sound.

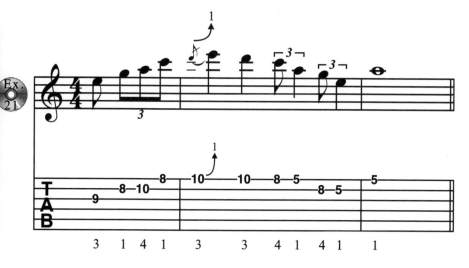

Let's put all these licks together for a complete blues thought. Be sure to play along with the example in the video.

Man, what an intense couple of licks! We've managed to cover a lot of ground. Remember that bending is a challenging technique. Take your time and use a solid approach to the fundamentals.

SOLO CONSTRUCTION

 n this lesson, we will have the first of many discussions on the topic of solo construction. First, we are going to learn about *target notes*. We will discuss what they are, where they are, and why they are so important. This is a really good "nuts-and-bolts" approach that you will use for the rest of this book. So, let's dig in.

Target Notes: Definition and Application

What is a target note? Simply put, it means the good notes in the scale, or the most important notes in the scale at that moment. The target-note approach is deep and vast. It grows as you grow. In this lesson, we'll cover the fundamentals so we can start using this potentially enormous idea. Let's listen to our A Minor Pentatonic Box #1.

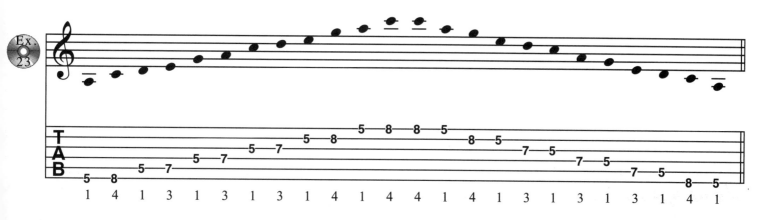

When we play the A Minor Pentatonic scale from bottom to top, it lacks focus and direction. But if we play it from octave to octave, the sound of the scale starts to emerge.

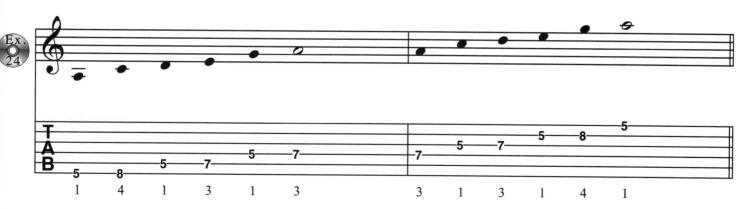

By starting and stopping on the A notes, we clearly define the scale's sound. We, in fact, targeted the A notes, or the root notes, of the A Minor Pentatonic scale. This is the basic idea. Ultimately, we want to be able to target any note in any scale, but for now, we'll concentrate on the most important target notes first.

Target Notes in A Minor Pentatonic

In our first exercise, we'll use our A Minor Pentatonic Box #1 and target the A notes.

Notice that the lick starts and stops on the A note. Also notice, at the end of this exercise, how we have to learn to target notes using our bends as well.

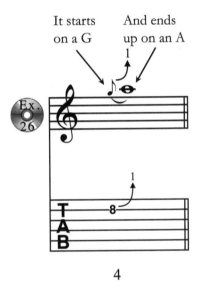

Remember to memorize where all of the A notes are in the first A Minor Pentatonic box. They are, in fact, the root notes of that pattern. The root note is the most important note in the scale and in the chord.

The 12-Bar Blues

The most common musical form used in the blues is what's known as the *12-bar blues*. It is a simple chord progression involving three dominant 7 chords occurring in a repeating pattern. These three chords are, of course, different depending on which key you are in, however, in order to refer to them across all keys, we identify these chords as I, IV, and V. The I chord is the dominant 7 chord whose root is the tonic of the key we are in. The IV chord is a dominant 7 chord whose root is a perfect 4th up from the tonic. The V chord is a dominant 7 chord whose root is a 5th higher than the tonic. Here is a quick reference chart of all the I-IV-V relationships available:

I	IV	V
A	D	E
A♯, B♭	D♯, E♭	E♯, F
B	E	F♯
C	F	G
C♯, D♭	F♯, G♭	G♯, A♭
D	G	A
D♯, E♭	G♯, A♭	A♯, B♭
E	A	B
F	B♭	C
F♯, G♭	B, C♭	C♯, D♭
G	C	D
G♯, A♭	C♯, D♭	D♯, E♭

Notes listed together in the same box are known as *enharmonic equivalents*. An enharmonic equivalent is a single pitch that is known by different note names depending on the situation or the key of the tune you are playing.

There are many variations of the 12-bar blues, including some that are highly sophisticated. However, the most common, and the one we will discuss in this book, goes like this: four bars of I, two bars of IV, two bars of I, one bar of V, one bar of IV, one bar of I, and one bar of V.

Here is the measure-by-measure form of the 12-bar blues:

| I | I | I | I | IV | IV | I | I | V | IV | I | V |

For example, here is a 12-bar blues progression in the key of A:

| A7 | A7 | A7 | A7 | D7 | D7 | A7 | A7 | E7 | D7 | A7 | E7 |

Targeting the Roots of the Chords

Target notes help us direct the focus of a lick or a melody. We can play the A Minor Pentatonic scale over a 12-bar blues in A, and for the most part, it works. However, it works better if we focus the scale to the actual chords. It sounds complicated, but really it's kind of simple. Let's break it down. If the band is playing a blues in A, and they're on the I chord, A7, we can use the notes from the A Minor Pentatonic Box #1 when soloing. Only this time, we'll start and stop on the A notes.

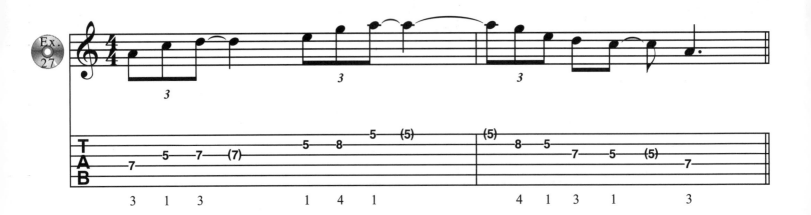

When the band moves on to the IV chord, D7, we'll keep following that box but focus on the D notes.

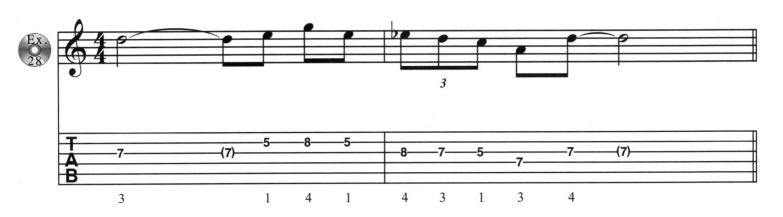

When the band goes to the V chord, E7, we'll stay on that box but focus on the E notes.

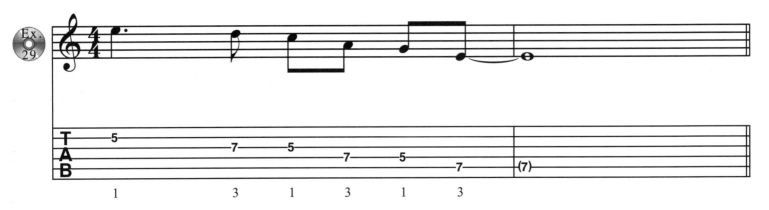

Notice how the scale has a different focus each time we change the target note.

A Blues Scale Targeting I, IV, and V

Following is another take on target notes. In this exercise, we'll play the *blues scale* in a descending fashion. A blues scale is the same as a pentatonic scale except it includes an additional note, the ♭5th.

Swing 8ths

Because the above lick lands on an A note, it would probably work best with the A7, which is the I chord.

Here's the same lick, but ending on a D note.

Swing 8ths

Notice how this totally changes the flavor. Because this lick targeted the D note, it would sound best with the D7, which is the IV chord.

This next lick does all the same stuff, but targets the E note. It works best with the E7, which is the V chord.

Swing 8ths

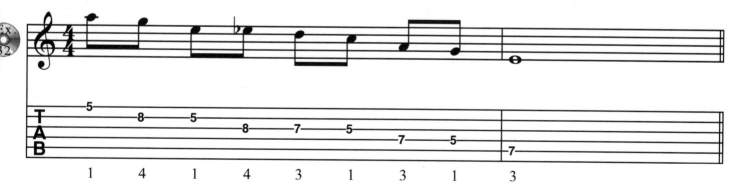

This is handy and useful stuff! Play all three licks in a row to really hear the difference. Then grab a friend and play these licks over a blues progression in A.

Pattern for Identifying the Minor Pentatonic

To have a real command of the target-note concept, we have to be able to spell and identify each note within a given scale. This kind of knowledge is the key to soloing freedom. We know how to target a note, but now we need to know how to find these notes quickly in the heat of battle. The quickest way is to simply memorize the note names for each step in the pattern. The following exercise will not only show us a method for memorizing the note names, but it will also give us some new notes in the pattern to target. We'll be using the A Minor Pentatonic Box #1 for this exercise. First, we play from A to A and spell each note out loud.

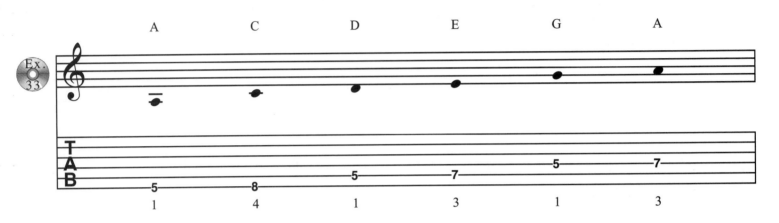

Then, we play from C to C and spell it out loud.

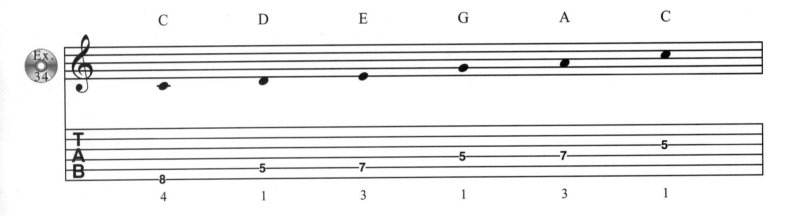

Then, we play from D to D and spell it out loud.

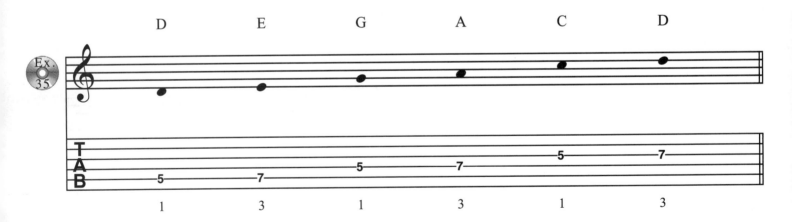

Continue this process through the entire pattern.

Let's master the pattern.

After you've mastered the pattern, play it while reciting the notes out loud.

TRILLS

For the next several lessons, we are going to be discussing soloing techniques. These are the little tricks that we use in our soloing to make the blues sounds that we love. In this lesson, we are going to learn all about *trills*. We will investigate this great-sounding technique, which utilizes hammer-ons and pull-offs, and learn a few new licks along the way.

Trills Explained

A trill is a musical ornament consisting of the rapid alteration between two notes, using a combination of consecutive hammer-ons and pull-offs. The trill is a sound we hear often in all types of guitar playing, not just blues. It's one of those great techniques that requires some practice before we can use it freely. Here's how it's done:

Let's use this   And this
C note.   D note.

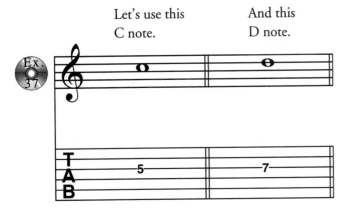

First, we'll play the C note and then hammer on to the D note, then immediately pull off the D back to the C note.

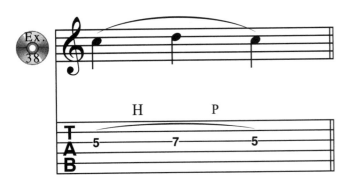

Once this technique feels comfortable, practice repeating it over and over.

And that's a trill! The cool thing about this type of trill is that you only have to pick the first note. The momentum of the hammer-ons and pull-offs keeps the string vibrating.

We can also flip it around and start on the D note, like this.

Let's play a couple of basic trills at a slow tempo. First, we'll play from C to D and then we'll play from D to C. Trills are typically played fast, but for this exercise, we'll treat them as eighth notes.

Trilling the Minor Pentatonic Box

Now, let's play trills over the A Minor Pentatonic Box #1. We're going to start on the A, 1st string, 5th fret, and hammer on to the C, 1st string, 8th fret. Then we'll turn that into a trill.

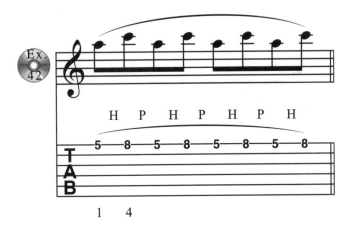

Next, move to the 2nd string and continue trilling.

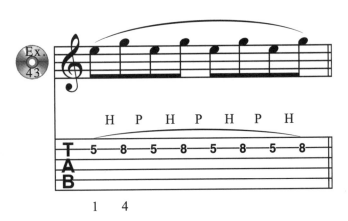

In moving to the next strings, just recall that box pattern to help you find the right notes. Here's the 3rd string.

Here's the 4th string.

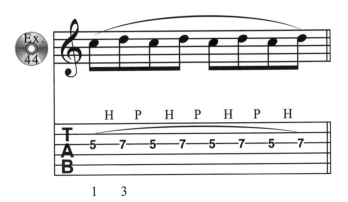

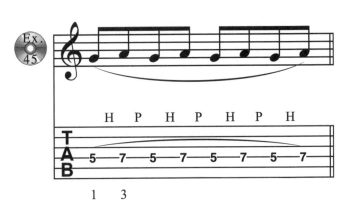

On the 5th string.

On the 6th string.

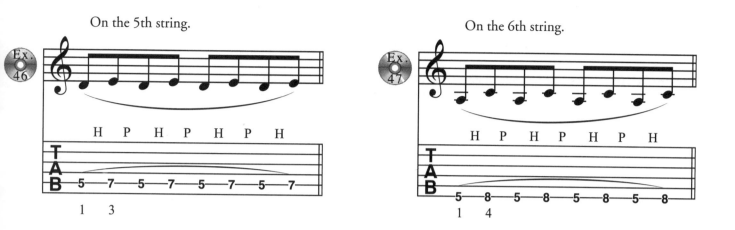

We have to remember to pick the first note every time we switch strings. Let's try this cool sound in tempo. Here again, this technique is meant to be played fast, but let's do it slowly first.

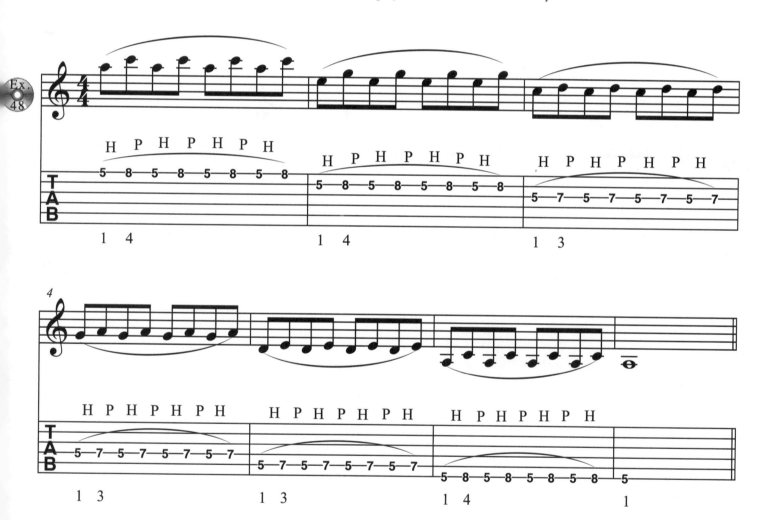

Trills and Licks

Let's learn two more licks featuring trills and the notes from the A Minor Pentatonic Box #1.

The first lick (measures 1 and 2 below) goes right down the scale and ends with a trill. However, this trill is a little different than those we've played before. It's played with a triplet feel. This can feel strange, because the fingerings are different on each downbeat. The second lick (measures 3 and 4 below) is all eighth notes, with a trill starting on the high note, then wrapping up with a nice bend.

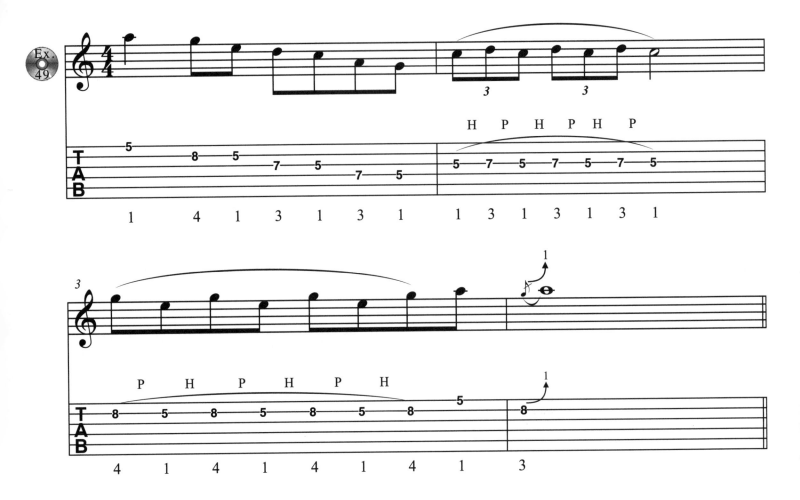

RETURN BEND TO PULL-OFF

In this lesson, we will be discussing the *return bend to pull-off* technique. This is another one of those great sounds in the blues guitar vocabulary that is a must. Guitarists like Jimi Hendrix, Stevie Ray Vaughan, and the three Kings (Freddie, Albert, and B. B.) used this in some form or another, and so should you! Let's learn this great technique so you can make it your own.

Return Bends Discussed

The return bend to pull-off is actually two techniques in one. It's a combination of the return bend (also known as the release bend) and the good-old pull-off. Let's tackle some of these various types of return bends first. Start by bending the following D note (3rd string, 7th fret) up to E.

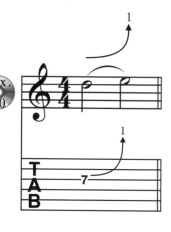

This is a whole-step bend, but when we relax the bend and bring it back to the D note, it is considered a return bend.

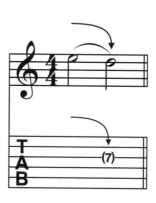

Remember this bending tip: Try to be dramatic when returning a bend, just like when we do a normal bend. In other words, make it sing.

Now, there are many other clever ways to do a return bend. Here are just a few.

We can bend up, hold it, and release it.

We can bend up, hold it, and then pick it again before we release it.

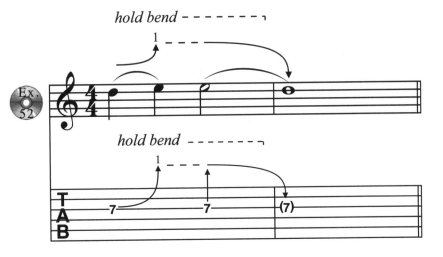

We can bend up, hold it, and then pick it several times as we release it. Note below that the indication "-½" tells you to release the bend enough to lower the pitch by a half step.

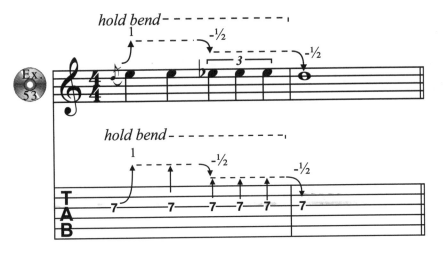

We can silently *pre-bend* the note and only release it. Pre-bending a note means to bend the string before picking it so that all that is heard is the release. The following example introduces the *one-and-a-half-step bend* (indicated by an arrow with a "1½" above it), which tells you to bend the note up a *minor 3rd*, or the distance of three frets.

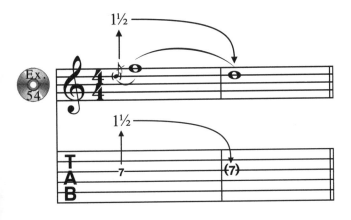

Playing Bends and Adding the Pull-Off

In this next exercise, we'll play through the different types of bends in succession.

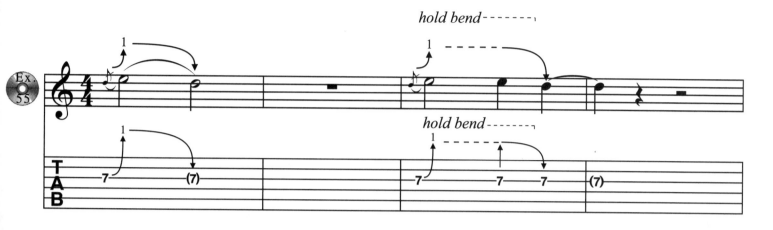

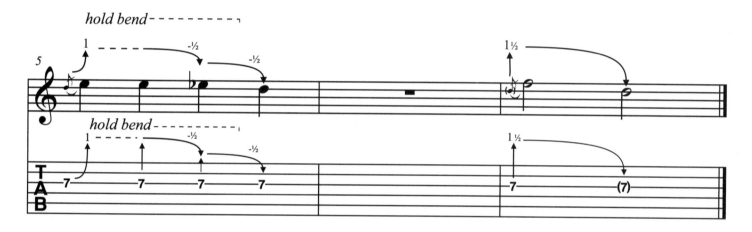

Now, let's combine pull-offs with our return bend to get a cool, new sound. This is a great technique for building phrases, and we'll check out a few examples. Below is the basic return bend to pull-off. Notice how, in this instance, we only pick the first note of the three-note phrase.

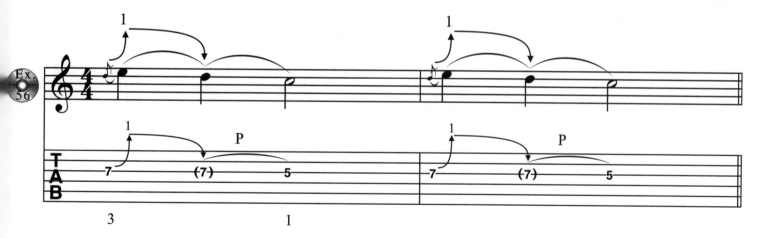

Pretty cool! Now, let's see what happens if we play the same thing several times in a row, a little faster.

Play these licks together at a slow tempo.

Creating Licks

Now, we're going to be creative and try using different types of return bends with different types of pull-offs. Let's play a couple of cool riffs using our new technique and the A Minor Pentatonic box patterns.

This first lick will be in the Box #2 fragment we discussed on page 12. We're going to start out with return bend to pull-off triplets on the 1st string, and then land on the root note A to wrap it up.

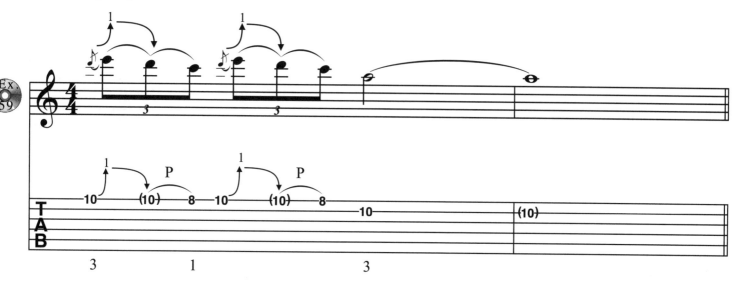

The next lick is similar to the previous one but is located in Box #1. We're going to play down the scale, then play a return bend to pull-off triplet and end up on the root note A.

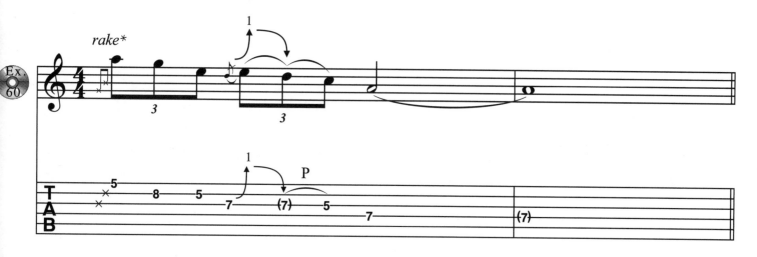

* The rake technique will be discussed in depth in the next lesson.

The two licks we just learned would sound great back-to-back in a blues solo. Let's try them together.

This is fun stuff that will really enhance your playing.

FORWARD RAKE

In this lesson, we are going to learn all about yet another great soloing technique, the *forward rake*. This is a really expressive tool used by most, if not all, blues guitarists to expand their dynamic and emotional range. It's a little difficult at first but, with some practice, the forward rake can become a big part of your blues vocabulary.

Muted Forward Rake Explained

The forward rake is a very expressive technique that requires us to mute with our right hand while raking down the strings with our pick.

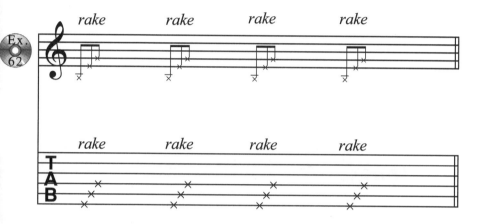

Now, the idea is to choose a note and rake as many strings as possible on the way to pick that note.

Instead of cleanly picking the note, we make it kind of greasy and rude by raking it.

Let's try a few muted forward rakes. We'll be using notes from A Minor Pentatonic Box #1.

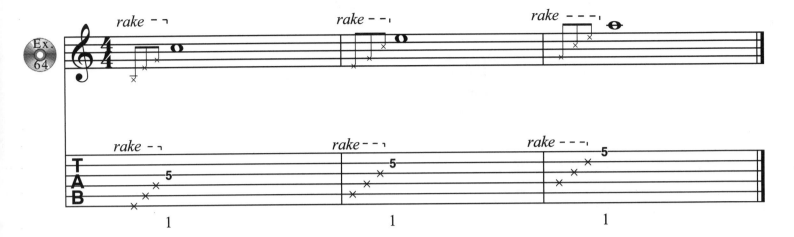

The Articulated Forward Rake

The *articulated forward rake* is a little bit different. Sometimes when we rake, we'll want to actually play some notes instead of just scratching the strings.

Instead of this:

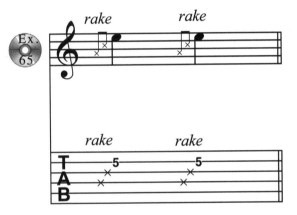

We might actually want to play some notes:

The idea with this type of rake is to use notes from the chord or scale to fill in where you would normally just scratch. Let's use an A Major triad and rake through it before bending our G note on the 8th fret of the 2nd string up a whole step to an A note. Notice that we have to loosen up our right-hand muting to let the notes sound out.

Licks with Rakes

Let's learn a few licks that make use of this powerful technique. We'll be playing out of the A Minor Pentatonic Box #1.

First we're going to rake into the C note on the 8th fret of the 1st string, and then play down the pattern to an E note on 5th fret of the 2nd string. Next, we'll rake into the G note on the 8th fret of the 2nd string. After that, we're going to rake into the G again, but this time bend it up a whole step to A.

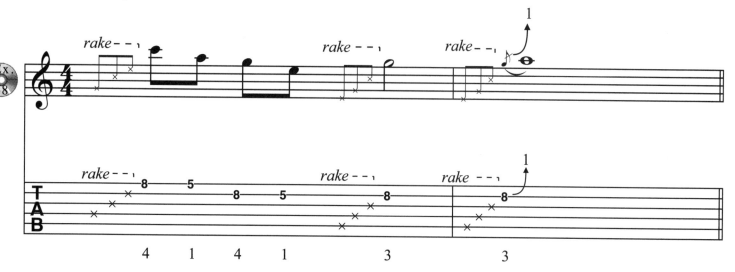

The next lick is a series of repeating triplets. First, we're going to rake into the D note on the 7th fret of the 3rd string, then bend up a whole step, quickly return it, and pull off to the C note on the 5th fret of the 3rd string. We'll do this four times in a row and wind it all up with an A note on the 4th string.

Now, let's play those licks back-to-back.

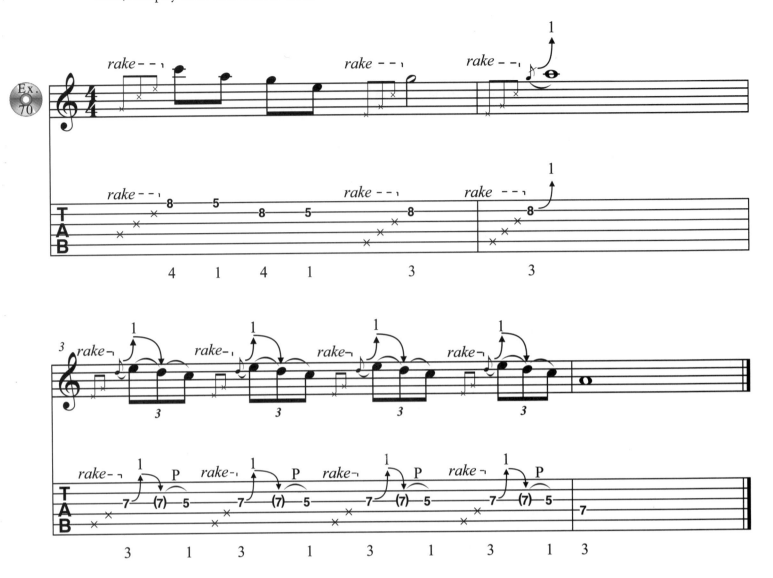

Raking is a really cool device that can be used in many different musical situations. It is an essential part of the blues vocabulary and must be mastered.

BASIC PHRASING

In this lesson, we are going to tackle the topic of *phrasing*. We are also going to check out a really cool pentatonic scale pattern.

When soloing, we seldom play an endless stream of notes. It's common to break things up with various short licks, rests, and so forth. How we arrange all of this solo material is referred to as phrasing. This can be thought of as the musical equivalent of speaking with your regular voice. In other words, phrasing is where we begin to learn how to speak with our guitar.

The 2nd A Minor Pentatonic Box

Before we can start talking about phrasing, let's have a look at A Minor Pentatonic Box #2.

Notice how this pattern picks up where Box #1 left off. Box #2 contains the same notes as Box #1, only in different locations. That means that we could use Box #2 instead of, or in addition to, Box #1. Let's spell it out as we go over the fingering. We're going to start with a C on the 8th fret of the 6th string.

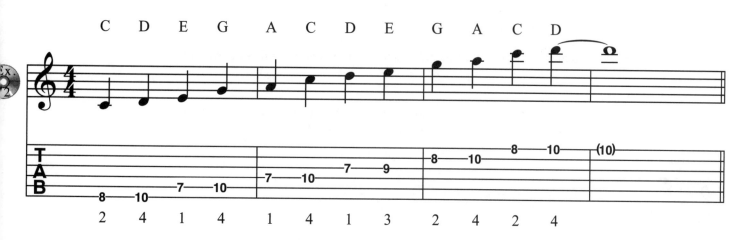

Learning How to Phrase

As mentioned before, phrasing is a lot like speaking. But before we can speak, we'll have to learn a few words in order to have something to say. We can think of a musical word as a phrase, and the way we assemble these words together into musical sentences is called phrasing. In the blues, there are tons of unique little phrases to learn and invent. Let's check some out right now.

All four of the following phrases use the A Minor Pentatonic Box #2. The first phrase starts on the C note on the 1st string, 8th fret and goes to an A note on the 2nd string, 10th fret. We repeat these two notes through the measure and wrap up with a nice bend from D to E on the 1st string, 10th fret.

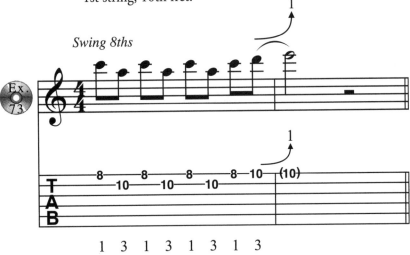

The next phrase is pretty much the same lick, only this time, we do not bend the last note. We simply land on the A note on the 2nd string, 10th fret.

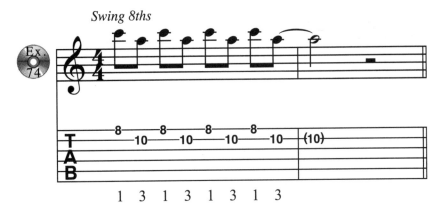

Notice how the two previous phrases complement each other in a kind of call-and-response fashion.

Our third phrase starts on a C note on the 1st string, 8th fret. We're going to play right down the scale pattern in eighth notes until we reach the C note on the 4th string, 10th fret.

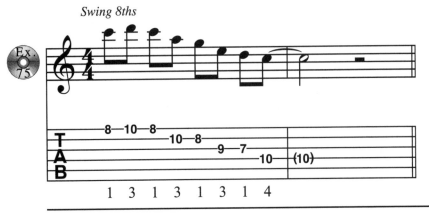

Our fourth phrase uses the same rhythm as the third phrase but with different notes. We start on the C note on the 10th fret of the 4th string, then we play an A note on the 7th fret of the 4th string. We're going to repeat these two notes an additional two times, then continue down the scale pattern to a G note on the 5th string, 10th fret. At the end, we'll land on an E on the 5th string, 7th fret.

These are some really good starting points for creating your own phrases. Try them in succession, as seen below, and be sure to play this exercise along with the video to ensure you are playing them correctly.

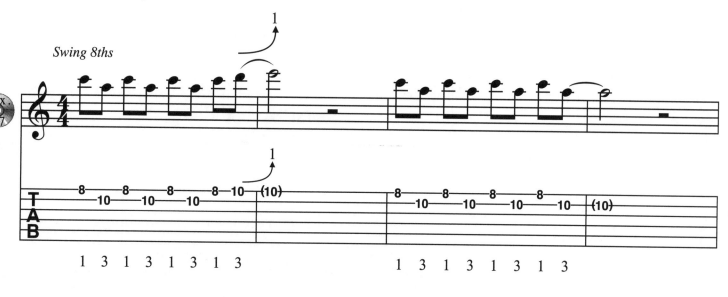

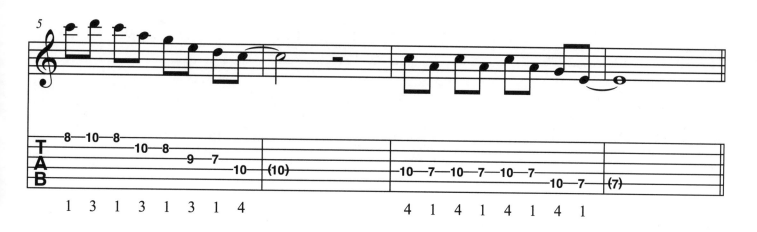

Phrasing Over a 12-Bar Blues

Now that we have a few phrases together, let's use them and a few new ones in a cool 12-bar solo.

Let's check it out, blow by blow. We're in the key of A Major. Over the first four measures, we'll use the phrases we learned in the previous lesson. Over measure 5, we play a new short phrase, and then answer it with a similar phrase in measure 6. Over measures 7 and 8, we play a phrase similar to the one we started with, only an octave lower. In measures 9–11, we use a repeating phrase throughout, changing only one note in each measure in order to target the chord roots as we learned in a previous lesson. Measure 12 has the same rhythm as the preceding three measures, but it uses different notes and does not involve the rake.

Remember, a phrase is your word. Phrasing is your sentence. Practicing these phrases will allow you to speak the universal language of music.

SIMPLE SLIDE EXERCISES

I n this lesson, we are going to investigate *sliding* and all of the wonderful things we can do with it. Sliding is a great way to move from position to position or just dress up an ordinary note. Many blues solos use this technique extensively. Without sliding, it would be very difficult to express yourself, especially in the blues.

Introducing Slides

Sliding is a great way to add a little fire to any situation. We can take a couple of notes and really spice them up with a few cool slides. There are so many ways to slide a note, but one thing is for sure: once sliding works its way into your technique, things really start to get lively. Let's check out some common slides.

Below, we're going to slide from a C note to a D note on the 1st string. We'll pick the C at the 8th fret, and while the note is still ringing, we'll slide it up to the D at the 10th fret.

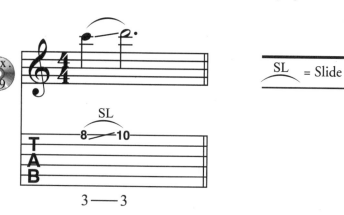

Now, let's reverse that, and pick the D and slide down to the C.

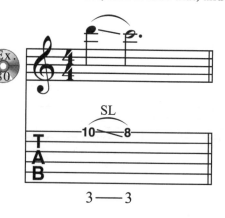

Let's play a few slides on a few different strings.

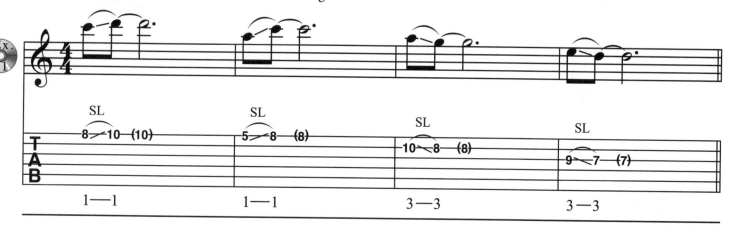

Creative Sliding

Creativity is the word of the day with sliding. Any note can be slid to or from anywhere on the fingerboard. So, let's do some creative sliding. Below, we're going to slide up the A Minor Pentatonic Box #1 and into Box #2. Starting on the lowest note on each string, pick and slide up to the next note. When we get to the 3rd string, we'll slide into Box #2 and continue the sliding pattern.

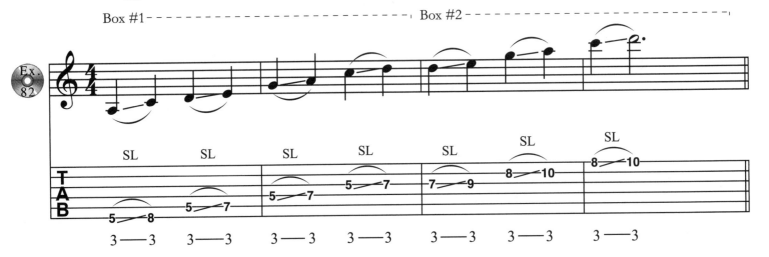

Adding Smoothness to Our Technique

Sliding is the basis for many a blues lick. It really adds to the smoothness of our technique. Here are a few common licks that use sliding. These licks are all played out of our pentatonic boxes and are really easy. Remember, it's always a good idea to play along with the video to reinforce your rhythm and technique.

Swing 8ths

As you can see, sliding is a lot of fun. Be creative with it and work it into your everyday playing.

MAJOR PENTATONIC VERSUS MINOR PENTATONIC

Having clear understanding and command of the major and minor pentatonic scales is essential to the blues player. This knowledge is the very foundation for conjuring up a variety of moods and colors in our playing. Over the next couple of lessons, we will begin our journey towards better pentatonic understanding to become that slammin' blues player that lives in us all. Let's start by learning about the *major pentatonic scale*. We'll analyze its construction and compare it to the minor pentatonic scale to observe their differences and similarities.

The Task at Hand

Pentatonic scales, both major and minor, are probably the most widely used scales in blues and rock. They are also common in many other musical styles as well. They're simple and accessible, generate thousands of musical melodies, and can serve as a springboard into more adventurous scale choices. They can also be a point of frustration and confusion until fully understood.

There are, as we are still discovering, different types of pentatonic scales. In fact, there are a whole variety of pentatonic scales that will fit a variety of musical situations, not to mention all of the custom-made pentatonic scales used by more advanced players. Pentatonic scale theory can be very complex and confusing, but fear not! We're going to take it slow and easy, collect only the knowledge that we need for the task at hand, and then move right on. Our goal over the next couple of lessons will be to get a clear understanding of the two most important pentatonic scales in existence: the major pentatonic and the minor pentatonic. Then, we're going to put them to work in the blues idiom. This newfound knowledge will serve as a foundation for future pentatonic exploration. Not to mention, it will also make you a pretty smokin' blues guitarist!

Comparing A Major and A Minor Box Patterns

Let's go over some quick basics before we play. The major pentatonic scale belongs to the major family of scales and chords, and the minor pentatonic scale belongs to the minor family of scales and chords. The word *pentatonic* translates, literally, to five tones: *penta* means five, and *tonic* refers to tones, or notes. The major pentatonic and minor pentatonic are two different scales, each containing five notes. It is a good idea to know the names of these notes. For this discussion, let's use A Major Pentatonic Box #2 and A Minor Pentatonic Box #1.

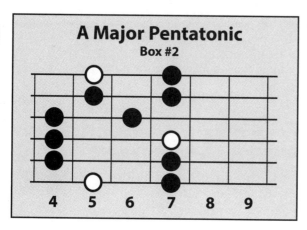

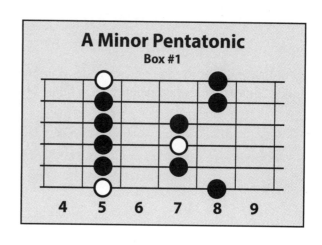

Now, let's recite the note names in each scale as we play both patterns from root to root. Our goal here is to observe what notes are the same, and what notes are different. Let's start with the A Minor Pentatonic Box #1 at the 5th position.

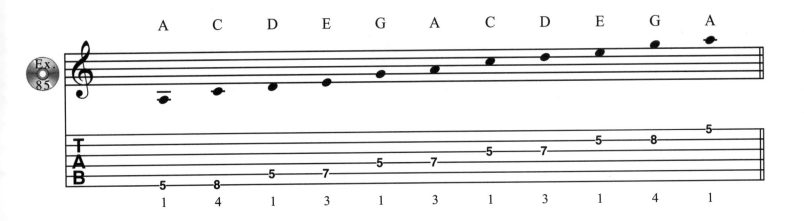

Now, let's check out the A Major Pentatonic Scale Box #2 starting at the 5th fret of the 6th string.

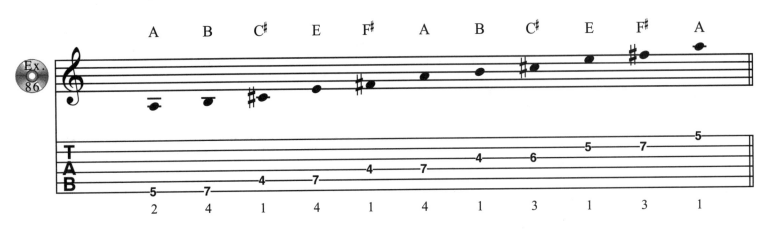

Now that you have the box patterns under your fingers, take some time to memorize the notes inside of them. This will certainly help in future blues endeavors.

Major and Minor Pentatonic Theory

Now that we've spelled the two scales, let's make some observations. When we spell an A Minor triad, we get the root, A, the 3rd, C, and the 5th, E.

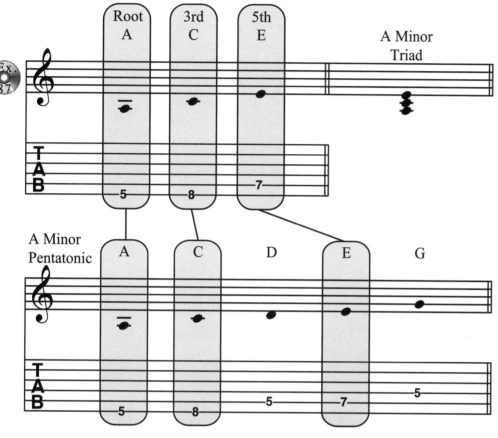

When we compare this to an A Minor Pentatonic scale, we notice that three of the five notes are the same as the A Minor triad. We have an A, which is the root, then a C, which is the minor 3rd, then a D, then an E, which is the 5th, then a G.

It works the same with the A Major triad as well. We have a root, A, the 3rd, which is C♯, and E, the 5th. Now, let's compare the A Major triad with the A Major Pentatonic scale. We have an A, which is the root, a B, a C♯, which is the 3rd, an E, which is the 5th, and then an F♯.

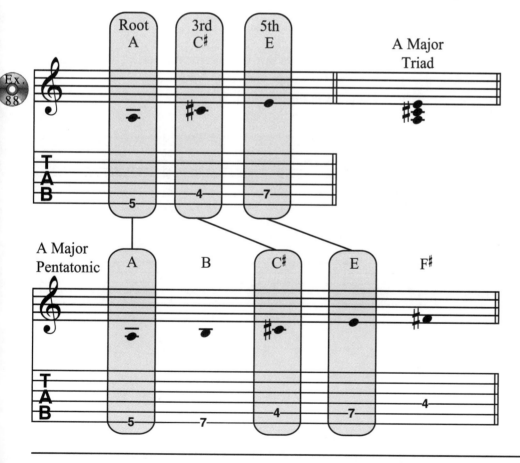

Here again, three of the five notes are the same.

Just like with chords, the major pentatonic scale has the natural 3rd (in this case, C♯) from its corresponding major triad. Likewise, the minor pentatonic scale has a ♭3rd (in this case, C) from its corresponding minor triad.

Now that we've opened up a confusing can of worms with way too much theory, here's the real point: We need scales at our command that define basic major and minor tonality, and major and minor pentatonic scales do just that. They contain just enough notes to outline the chord without confusing the sound. The major pentatonic scale fits the major chord like a glove, and the minor pentatonic scale does the same for the minor chord. Major and minor chords are the gateway to more complex chords like dominant 7 and minor 7 chords. Pentatonic scales function the same way. At the core of many complex scale sounds are major or minor pentatonic scales. Wow, now that our brain is completely on fire, let's move on to something that we can put our hands on.

Accompanying Yourself with Chords

In this exercise, we will accompany ourselves with chords and play the pentatonic scale over them. First, play a 6th-string-root A Minor barre chord.

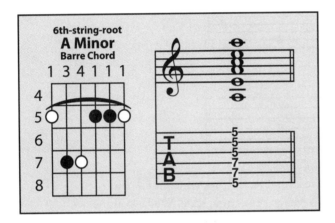

Let your ear soak up the sound of the chord. Play the A Minor Pentatonic Box #1 from the A at the 5th fret of the 1st string down to the A on the 7th fret of the 4th string. Then play the chord once again. Notice how the chord and the scale seem to complement one another.

The major chord works the same way. Play a 6th-string-root A Major chord.

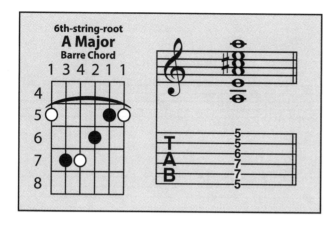

Play the A Major Pentatonic Box #2 from the A on the 5th fret of the 1st string, down to the A on the 7th fret of 4th string and compare that to the A Major chord.

Fits just like a glove!

Multiple Scales Over One Chord

In blues, it's okay to use a minor pentatonic or blues scale with a major chord, or more precisely, a *dominant 7* chord (which consists of the root, 3rd, 5th, and minor 7th). We just learned how to access a major pentatonic scale for a major chord, but this scale will also work with the dominant version of the same chord. What's this? Two different scales to play over the same chord? This is where the blues really starts to get interesting. Let's play an A Blues Scale Box #1 and an A Major Pentatonic Scale Box #2 over an A7 6th-string-root barre chord.

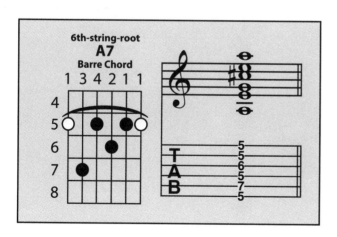

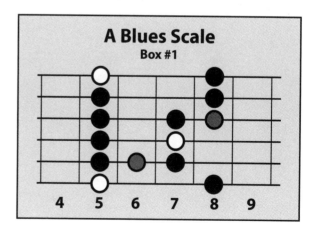

This is very similar to the previous exercise. First, we'll play the A7 chord. Then, we're going to play the Blues scale Box #1 down from the A on the 5th fret of the 1st string to the next available A on the 7th fret of the 4th string.

Now, let's do the same thing with the A Major Pentatonic Box #2. We're going to play the A7 chord, then the scale from root to root.

Although we're just scratching the surface, this exercise pretty much lays the groundwork for much of our upcoming blues maneuvers. In upcoming lessons, we'll be learning how to effectively combine these scales.

INTRODUCTION TO OVERLAPPING BOXES

In blues, many of the rules of traditional music theory are cast aside. Blues music is in fact a type of folk music created by regular people, not rocket scientists, so the sounds are simple, elegant, and homegrown. How to arrive at these awesome sounds can be pretty easy if you know the tricks. In this lesson, we're going to begin learning about overlapping pentatonic boxes and how to use them.

Review

In the blues, it is very common to shift from major pentatonic to minor pentatonic, or vice versa. There are some specific, time-honored places in the blues form where these shifts occur, but we're going to save that for the next lesson. In this lesson, we're going to concentrate on the fingerboard aspects of shifting through our two pentatonic sounds. After we get more comfortable managing this stuff on the fingerboard, tackling the various applications will be a breeze. Let's do a little bit of a review before we get started. Remember, the A Minor Pentatonic Box #1 and #2 have the very same shape as the A Major Pentatonic Box #1 and #2. There are only two real differences: one, they are in different locations on the neck, and two, the roots, in this case the A notes, are in different locations in relation to the actual shape of the patterns. For an explanation, see the diagrams below.

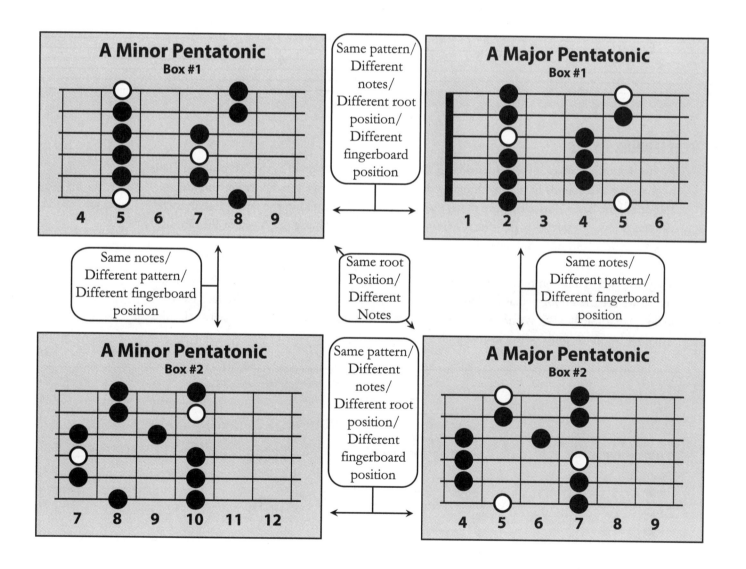

Overlapping Major and Minor Pentatonic

In our first exercise, we're going to play a few lines that move up the fingerboard through our pentatonic boxes. The goal here is to get comfortable moving around the neck and absorb the sound of the A Major Pentatonic mingling with the A Minor Pentatonic. Also, take note of where these patterns overlap.

We're going to start out with the A Major Pentatonic Box #1 on the A at the 2nd fret of the 3rd string and play all the way up the box. When we get to the A note at the 5th fret of the 1st string, we slide it up to the B note one step higher, putting us in A Major Pentatonic Box #2. Then, we shift gears and go down the A Minor Pentatonic Box #1, starting at the highest note, C, at the 8th fret of the 1st string. From here, we're going to play down the box for four notes. Then, we jump up to the A Minor Pentatonic Box #2 via the E at the 9th fret of the 3rd string to complete the line.

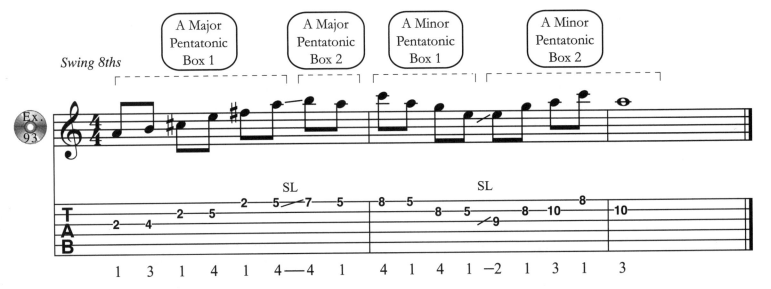

Overlapping Boxes

In this section, let's pay specific attention to where the patterns overlap at the 5th position. This is where the two sounds have something in common, something we can attach our thinking to and call home base. Notice that the roots, the A notes, are all located in the same place in each pattern. So we can safely say that the A Minor Pentatonic Box #1 and the A Major Pentatonic Box #2 share a common root location.

They also share common root locations with the A 6th-string-root barre chord at 5th position. Just as we use the minor pentatonic box #1 as our main minor pentatonic pattern, let's use the major pentatonic box #2 as our main major pentatonic pattern. This will be especially helpful when we begin to combine the scale sounds.

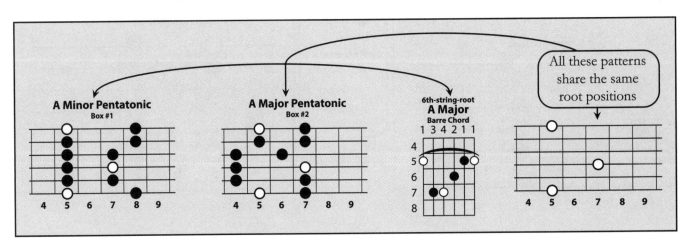

In the following exercise, we'll play something similar to the last exercise, only this time, we're going to stay in 5th position. You just play up the A Major Pentatonic Box #2, starting on the A at the 7th fret of the 4th string, then play down the A Minor Pentatonic Box #1, starting at the highest note C at the 8th fret of the 1st string.

Swing 8ths

4 1 3 1 3 1 3 1   4 1 4 1 3 1 3 1 3

Adding the Blues Scale to the Mix

Let's continue to find and add the blue notes to our go-to patterns at the 5th position. These two patterns will become very valuable to you, so spend some extra time with them. We have already covered the blues scale, in which notes are added to the minor pentatonic scale to give it that blues flavor. When blue notes are added to the major pentatonic scale, we get what is sometimes called the *country scale*.

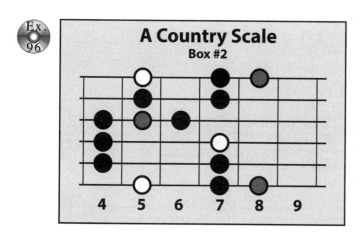
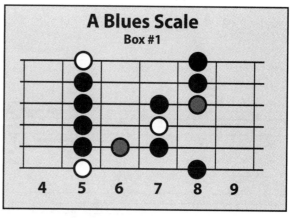

This next exercise is almost the same as the last one, only this time, we add the blue notes to the boxes. We'll go up the A Country Scale Box #2 then down the A Blues Scale Box #1.

Swing 8ths

4 1 2 3 2 4 2 4   1 4 1 4 3 1 3 1 3

Okay, very cool. Now, we're getting to the real essence of the blues sound: the interplay between the major and minor pentatonic.

PHRASING

Now that we have a firm grip on major and minor pentatonic scales, we can start to put this stuff to work. In this lesson, we're going to learn a cool 12-bar solo that shifts through our new pentatonic scale sounds. While we are here, let's also learn some cool tips and suggestions on how to make good scale choices while soloing.

12-Bar Blues in A Combining Major and Minor: Full Solo and Measures 1–4

As briefly mentioned in our last lesson, there are some time-honored locations in the blues form where we might shift from one pentatonic sound to another. Let's explore some of the common moves that occur in the 12-bar blues form by breaking one down into four-bar sections. Here is the whole thing together.

Full Solo

Measures 1–4

Remember, on measures 1–4 of the 12-bar blues, we stay on the I chord, which, in this case is A7. We use the A Major Pentatonic Box #2 for all four measures. Start out with a *pickup* line on the "&" of beat 3 followed by a short phrase. (Note: A pickup is a note or group of notes that occur before the first complete measure.)

Then, we repeat the same phrase heading into measure 3, only this time, let's change the last note to make it interesting.

In this phrase, we will utilize *quarter-step bends*. A quarter-step bend is similar to a half-step bend, but instead of bending the note up a half step (the distance of one fret), the note is only bent half of that distance. What this means is, by playing a less extreme bend, we achieve a pitch in between the two pitches of neighboring frets.

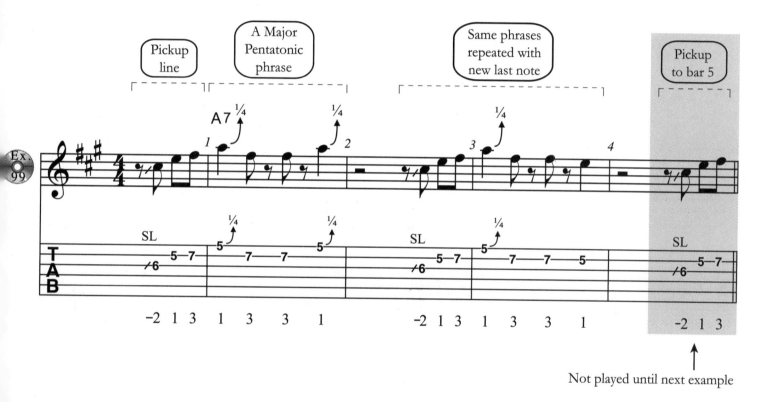

Not played until next example

Measures 5–8

Things start to get interesting in measures 5–8. In measures 5–6, while on the IV chord, D7, we will use the A Blues Scale Box #1. We'll play a short phrase that rhythmically mimics the opening phrases, but with a different scale; this time, after the three pickup notes, we're going to start on C at the 5th fret of the 3rd string and follow the box. Then, we play a descending run starting on the E at the 5th fret of the 2nd string.

This leads us into measures 7 and 8, where we go back to the I chord, A7, and back to the A Major Pentatonic Box #2.

Then, after landing squarely on the A note at the 7th fret of the 4th string, we will continue this little phrase with the time-honored minor 3rd to major 3rd slide between the C at the 5th fret of the 3rd string and the C♯ a half step higher. This occurs on the "&" of beat 2.

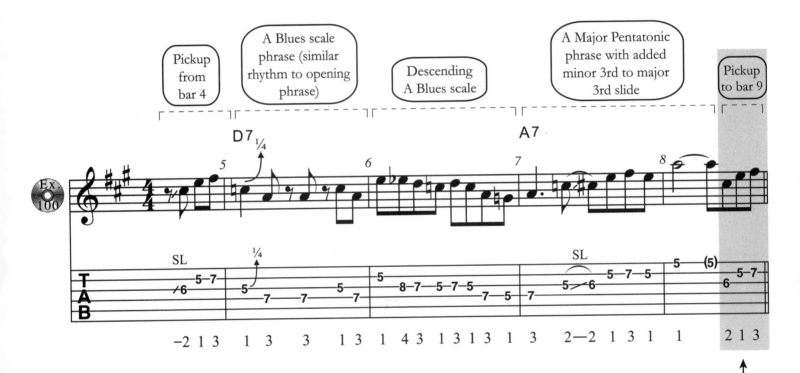

Not played until next example

Measures 9–12

Measures 9–12, the last four measures, are known as the *turnaround*. This is the part of the 12-bar blues where the V chord is involved. During the turnaround the soloist plays a phrase that wraps up the form and takes the listener back to the beginning. This is a signature part of playing the blues and great blues guitarists distinguish themselves with many unique approaches to this part of the solo.

On measure 9, we're on the V chord, E7. We'll cross between the major and minor pentatonic for this phrase. We're going to start at G on the 8th fret, 2nd string which comes from A Minor Pentatonic, but then we'll quickly switch to A Major Pentatonic.

Then, for measure 10, we're on the IV chord, D7. Let's use the Blues Box #1 for this phrase. We're going to start on the D note at the 7th fret, 3rd string and then blues it up.

Then, for measure 11, we're on the I chord, A7. Let's go to the A Major Pentatonic Box #2 for this one. Also, we'll throw in our minor 3rd to major 3rd slide lick for extra blues flavor.

Measure 12 goes to the V chord, E7, on the "&" of beat 1. Let's punctuate that quick change with a simple E note at the 5th fret, 2nd string.

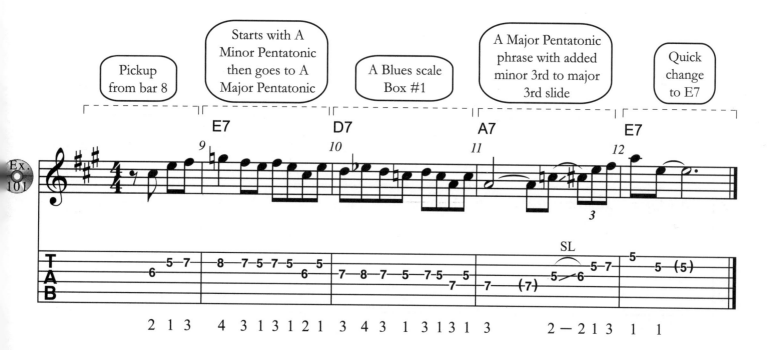

When you feel comfortable with the four-bar phrases we just covered, go back and play the complete solo.

Conclusion

What scale to play with what chord seems to be the age-old question. In blues, nothing is really etched in stone, especially scale usage. Having said that, I would like to offer up a few no-brainer tips that might help. Do not overthink these suggestions, just use them. The theoretical aspects will reveal themselves in due time, and remember, these are not rules, just suggestions.

In the blues, minor pentatonic scales work great in major keys, but major pentatonic scales do not work well in minor keys.

While on the I7 chord, use a major pentatonic. While on the IV7, use the minor pentatonic with the root in the key of the blues you are playing. While on the V7, use either or both pentatonic scales, and don't forget to extend these sounds to the blues and country pentatonic scales. Refer to the chart below for an easy guide to these scale suggestions, which are also demonstrated in the key of A.

SCALE SUGGESTIONS (What Scale to Play over What Chord)		
I7	**IV7**	**V7**
major pentatonic scale	minor pentatonic scale	major pentatonic scale minor pentatonic scale blues scale country scale
In the Key of A		
A7	**D7**	**E7**
A Major Pentatonic scale	A Minor Pentatonic scale	A Minor Pentatonic scale A Major Pentatonic scale A Blues scale A Country scale

Great job, and thanks for joining us for these lessons. Be sure to check out the other titles in the Serious Blues series, and keep jamming!